And Baby Makes Three, Now What Do We Do?

The step-by-step guide to taking care of your new baby

By Suzanne Doyle-Ingram

And Baby Makes Three: Now What do we do?

ISBN 0-9737453-0-4

Prominence Publishing

www.prominencepublishing.com

Disclaimer

I, Suzanne Doyle-Ingram, am not a physician, nor do I have experience in the field of medicine at all. I am simply an experienced mother. Everything in my books, that I personally provide is based on my experience with the challenges of parenting a new baby.

My book, my website and any other materials I provide, either electronically or on paper are not meant to be a substitute for individualized medical evaluation, advice, care, or recommended treatment from a qualified, licensed health professional. Each child is different. I know my daughters and son, but I do not know my readers' children. Parents are strongly urged to consult with their child's physician prior to adopting anything suggested in this book or on my website.

Table of Contents

Chapter 1: Introduction..7

Chapter 2: Our Struggle with Our First Baby 11

Chapter 3: The Marathon of Labor 15

Chapter 4: You Already are a Great Parent 17

What Great Parents Do 18

Chapter 5: Getting Set Up..21

What You Need 21

What you don't need 28

Setting Up Your Nursing Station.......................29

Chapter 6: Your First Day Home 33

The Outfit..33

The Car Seat 34

Talk to Your Baby..34

In the car on the way home 36

Chapter 7: Arriving Home..39

Safety First 40

Chapter 8: Giving Your Baby a Bath 43

Getting Ready for the bath..................................43

Supplies..44

Start the bath 45

Chapter 9: For Crying Out Loud!............................49

The 5 Causes of Crying:.......................................49

#1 Hunger...50

#2 Dirty diaper..51
#3 Gas...51
#4 Lonely...52
#5 Tired or over stimulated 52

Crying Checklist...52
#1. Is it her diaper? 53
#2. Is she hungry? 53
#3. Does she need to burp?...........................53
#4. Does she need a change of scene?............54
#5. Is she tired? 54
#6. Does she need to suck?............................54

Chapter 10: Fifteen Surefire Ways to Calm Crying..**57**
1. Tour Guide 57
2. Bobbing for baby 57
3. Change artist 58
4. White Noise 58
5. Hum 58
6. Five S's (or 4 S's and one J)......................59
7. Couch potato 59
8. Touchy Feely..59
9. Water Baby..59
10. Rock on..60
11. Hold tight 60
12. Let's swing! 61
13. Swing it more! 61
14. Wanna go for a ride? 61
15. Forget it 61

Chapter 11: The Pacifier Debate **63**
Some of the benefits of pacifiers.........................64
Some of the disadvantages of pacifiers..............64
Getting Rid of the Pacifier 65

Chapter 12: Sleep...**67**

The Ten Commandments of Sleep: 68

Why Babies Wake Up...70

How to put your baby down when she's
asleep (and keep her that way) 71

How to Swaddle..73

Chapter 13: All About Breastfeeding **75**

Benefits..75

My experience breast feeding Hana 77

Give your baby 40 days....................................79
  Establishing a good milk supply 79
  Positioning...81
  Engorgement...83

Sore Nipples 85

Signs That Breastfeeding is Going Well 85

Chapter 14: The Truth about Formula.................**87**

Chapter 15: Breast Pump Basics **95**

Making Pumping Easier....................................96

**Chapter 16: Your life is about to change
completely** **99**

A typical day in the life of a new parent 99

Chapter 17: Frequently Asked Questions..........**107**

Chapter 18: Conclusion **115**

About The Author...**117**

Resources **119**

The Best baby books.......................................119

Websites: 121

Chapter 1: Introduction

This book is intended as a manual for all first-time parents tackling the challenge of bringing home their new baby yet having no idea how best to take care of them.

Not long ago, a new mother's mother used to come to stay with her and help her learn all about caring for her new baby; unfortunately, nowadays it is often not possible or simply not an option.

New parents are usually alone and have to figure it all out by themselves.

The thing is, you *will* figure it all out, and you *will* be a great parent!

But sometimes it's nice to have the tips and tricks upfront. I intend to help you by giving you resources on:

- Fifteen ways to calm your baby's crying (some that you have probably never heard of!)
- How to figure out *why* your baby is crying
- Lists of supplies you need and what you *really don't need*

- Practical advice on setting up a breastfeeding station
- How to show your baby the respect she deserves
- Overview of where your baby should sleep
- Tips on how to get your baby to sleep and stay asleep
- A typical day with a newborn
- Frequently Asked Questions

My name is Suzanne Doyle-Ingram and I am the mother of two daughters and one son, and I've been married for almost 20 years to my wonderful husband James Ingram.

I have a Bachelor of Arts degree in Linguistics and my work history ranges from educating and training to working as the Director of Operations for a major print publication. I currently own two businesses, both related to marketing and pubishing.

Our first child, Hana, was born in August 2001, after a fairly uneventful pregnancy (apart from the usual heartburn, bloody noses, swollen feet – you know how it is!) and a very straightforward all natural labor and delivery.

Suddenly we were a family of three! She was such a beautiful baby; we named her Hana, which means "flower" in Japanese.

All throughout my pregnancy I read every single book on pregnancy that I could get my hands on. My husband, James, used to tease me that I had my PhD in pregnancy.

While this book is here to help you cope with the immediate challenges of a newborn baby, I urge you to read a couple of others to balance out your preparation, especially if you are planning to breastfeed. There are some very good books out there; and I will recommend some to you. (See Resources at the end of this book).

However, none of the many books I read prepared me for Hana's non-stop crying. I so wished for a book that would tell me exactly what to do when she was screaming at 3:00am (and 4:00am and 5:00am...) and we couldn't settle her.

James and I really did not know what to do. We learned through trial and error what worked and what didn't, and I intend to lend you all our tools and tricks so that you never have to feel exasperated and helpless like we did.

What we needed was a book like this one – one that says, "If your baby is doing this, try this" and pinpoints exactly what to do.

Chapter 2: Our Struggle with Our First Baby

I knew instinctively that Hana definitely had something wrong with her. Unlike colic, which supposedly lasts 3 months, Hana cried pretty much non-stop for eight months. Eventually I figured out why (which I will explain later) but it was terribly stressful and just plain awful for us until then.

She was happy occasionally, don't get me wrong, but she cried consistently for six straight hours each evening from 6:00pm to midnight and then off and on during the day as well. When she woke up in the middle of the night to nurse, it would take an hour or two to get her back to sleep.

She also had eczema so badly that her skin would bleed. Sometimes James and I had to sleep with her in between us and each of us would hold one of her hands so she would not scratch and scratch and make herself bleed. Even when we put little mitts on her hands, she just pulled them off. We had no sleep and we were utterly miserable.

What's really sad is that my friends and family didn't really know this was going on. This was our first baby so we didn't know what to expect.

I would mention, "I'm so tired; Hana was up all night" but everyone *expects* you to be tired when you have a new baby. My poor sister-in-law now says that she will always feel guilty about not helping us more.

But really, I was so sleep-deprived and out-of-it that I didn't ask for help. I know now that I should have said, "I need HELP. Can I count on you to come over today from 12:00 to 2:00 and take Hana out in her stroller so I can get some sleep?" If that person said no, I should have called someone else and kept asking until I got help.

I was so tired that I really should not have been driving a car. I would close my eyes at red traffic lights and sleep for 30 seconds at a time!

Let me stop here for a moment. I want you to know that it is *very unusual* for a baby to cry as much as Hana did, so please don't let our story frighten you. Just know that we became experts at figuring out how to calm a crying baby. We know firsthand how stressful a crying baby can be and we will teach you all of our techniques to calm your baby. And if you do have a "high needs" baby, I want you to know that you are not alone. And it does not last forever.

Luckily, Hana completely changed at eight months old (I'll tell you how) and started sleeping 12 hours straight at night. It was awesome! Life was beautiful! And now (as of this edition in 2015) she is a wonderful, delightful (and eczema-free) fourteen-year-old. She is a kind, funny kid who is a pleasure to be around.

Alexa, our second child

Even during this difficult time with Hana, we always knew we wanted to have more children and we were blessed with our second daughter in March 2004.

We named her Alexa. This kid practically came out smiling! It was incredible! She hardly ever cried.

There was nothing we did differently with her; we were just lucky. (If one more person says, "It must be because you are less anxious with the second child" I'm going to scream!)

It just goes to show you how different kids can be.

But really "easy" kids are also challenging in some ways too, which sounds strange but it's true. The tips in this book will help you no matter what kind of baby you have.

Trey, our third child

One day, when Hana was about 4 years old, she looked over at Alexa and nonchalantly said, "Mommy has a baby in her tummy."

I whipped my head around to face her and said, "What did you say??" And she repeated, "Mommy has a baby in her tummy." I said, "No, honey, I don't have a baby in my tummy. Just because I am a little bit pudgy around the middle does not mean that I'm pregnant. Lots of mommies look like this. I am NOT pregnant."

She was furious. She was looking at me with this absolute look of fury on her little face. Her fists tightened and she screamed at me, "Yes you DO have a baby in your tummy! AND IT'S A BOY!!!" And with that, she stomped her tiny foot on the ground and stormed off.

I thought she was just being silly, and I figured that maybe someone at her daycare was having a baby or something. But a few weeks later, I found out I was indeed pregnant – 8 weeks along! She was right!

We had a beautiful baby boy and we named him Trey, meaning "third". (What can I say? I was exhausted and couldn't come up with anything else).

ϩ

"Before I got married I had six theories about bringing up children; now I have six children, and no theories."

~John Wilmot

Chapter 3: The Marathon of Labor

What is it really like to go through labor? Do you really want to know the truth? I will tell you. If you don't want to know what it's really like, then skip to the next section.

I have an analogy that I like to use to illustrate what pregnancy, labor, and parenthood is like that I will share with you.

Imagine you are planning to run a marathon. You train hard for it, eat right, do your exercises, and finally the big day arrives. You feel prepared and excited, but a bit nervous too. And you're off!

You run the marathon, getting progressively more and more tired, you fall once and skin your knee, but you keep going and going. Several times you want to quit, but those around you keep saying, "You can do this! Keep going! Just a little bit longer..." and at last you finally cross the finish line.

Congratulations! You've just completed a marathon! You are completely exhausted, you feel like you've been hit by a truck, your body hurts all over, you're sweating, bleeding, and limping.

But wait! Did you forget that you were supposed to start that new full-time job today?

Hurry, you're going to be late. Look, there's your new office right over there across from the Finish Line. You go over, still sweaty, bloody, and limping, and you are shown to your desk. You don't even get to have a shower.

You are supposed to know what you are doing at this new job but there is no employee manual and no one around. People are coming by your desk, demanding things from you in a foreign language and you have no idea what's going on.

This is what I felt like after I had Hana. I wish I could have had a tiny break between labor and being a parent. Doesn't that sound funny?! You're just so exhausted and in one split second you go from pregnant to parent. Don't worry, the hormones do kick in and you begin to feel excited and happy... eventually.

Chapter 4: You Already are a Great Parent

All throughout your pregnancy you took great care of your baby. You didn't drink alcohol or take any unnecessary medications. You probably exercised, didn't take Jacuzzi baths, and you didn't eat sushi, or Caesar salad, or raw oysters for that matter.

All the things that you "gave up" during pregnancy demonstrate what a great parent you already are!

You have been selfless and loving toward your baby.

The fact that you are reading this book shows how much you love your baby and that you want nothing but the best for your baby. Good for you!

You already are a great parent. **Believe it.**

Sometimes, just knowing that you *can* be a great parent makes you one. I used to teach literacy skills to people in my community and train volunteers as well. I always told the volunteers that the first thing you have to do is teach someone that they *can read*; that they *are able to learn to read*, and then you teach them how to read.

More than half the battle is teaching the confidence, and that has to come first.

A few days after your baby is born, you will be surprised to learn how much you already know about her!

You'll hear yourself saying to a visitor, "She likes it if you hold her like this…"

It may be hard to believe now, but no one will know your baby better than you.

You'll be the expert!

Several of my friends were nervous when they were pregnant about what kind of parents they would be. They weren't sure if they were "cut out for it". It makes me smile now when they say, ***"I'm an AWESOME mom!!"*** as they are making coffee, sorting laundry and holding the baby all at the same time.

What Great Parents Do

Great parents are calm and in control.

Let me repeat that: ***Great parents are calm and in control.***

As your child gets older, if you let her think she's the boss, forget ever getting her to listen to you, or respect you.

As our good friend Dan once told James and me, "Your kids are not your friends. They can be your friends when they're 25, but until then, you have to be the boss."

Great parents calmly guide their children through life, teaching them how to sleep, how to eat, how to dress themselves, how to play, how to share... essentially you have to teach them everything.

Consider this: Your "job" as a parent is to make yourself unemployed.

Chapter 5: Getting Set Up

In terms of "stuff" you need for the baby, the following outlines what you will need, and what you don't need.

What You Need

- Diaper rash ointment - I do not use diaper cream after every change. If necessary, I recommend using an all natural one. Of course the old standby Vaseline works great too.

- 2 packages of disposable diapers (I would get one size Newborn and one size 1. Your baby might quickly outgrow the newborn ones or never fit them at all)

- Or two dozen cloth diapers - even if you are totally committed to using cloth (I was for my first baby too!) do yourself a favor and buy a small number of disposables as well. I found that my newborns would wake up every time they peed when wearing cloth and that was every 20 minutes! Also, the cloth ones are sometimes too big for a newborn.

- Baby wipes – I didn't use store-bought wipes on Hana very often. I felt that she didn't need any propylene glycol, tocopheryl acetate, disodium cocoamphodiacetate, polysorbate 20, disodium phosphate, 2-bromo-2-nitropropane-1, 3-diol, and last but not least, iodopropynyl butylcarbamate on her perfect, soft bottom. I just bought a couple of yards of flannel fabric, cut them into squares and every day I would put a fresh bowl of warm water beside her change table. I would wipe her bottom with clean water after every change and place the used wipe in a diaper pail and then launder them in hot water and bleach. I have to admit, when she pooped, I used what I call the "chemical wipes", and then rinsed with water. She never got a bad diaper rash.

- Note: You do not need to spend your money on expensive Ivory Snow or any other "gentle" baby laundry soap. Just use a small amount of regular laundry soap and do a double rinse.

- Gentle baby soap - You really don't have to use soap on your newborn baby because they can't even get dirty! I just used plain old water for the first few weeks. Sometimes I would use a tiny bit of soap on the "Extra dirty" bits. I also like the liquid soaps they have now that can be used as baby body wash or shampoo. Check out the smell first before you buy it! My daughter gags at the smell of lavender.

- Baby shampoo – You don't really need to use shampoo for the first while either, but I do like the smell. Note: If your baby gets cradle cap (scaly, yellow flakes on her scalp), don't agonize over it. It is painless and usually goes away by itself. You can help it disappear by rubbing all natural oil (like olive oil) on it and carefully remove the flakes with your fingernail. Then shampoo all the oil out.

- 2-4 pacifiers - you should sterilize them beforehand so they are ready to go in the middle of the night. (See Pacifier Debate later in this book.) If you never need them, that's great. But if you do really need a pacifier to calm your little one in the middle of the night, you will be *deliriously happy* that you had the foresight to get them ready in advance. Our friends Shawnna and Darren gave us many presents before Hana was born, and one of the things they gave us was a pacifier. And I remember thinking at the time, "Well! I don't think I will be using this!" (all high and mighty...) And then one night, at about three in the morning, I was exhausted and breastfeeding constantly and I looked over at James and said, "What's the reason for not using a pacifier?" and neither of us could remember. We sterilized that pacifier, shoved it in Hana's mouth, and never looked back! She loved it, and often it was

all she needed to fall fast asleep. I swear by them!

- Blunt baby nail scissors or clippers - those little nails get so long and so sharp at an amazing speed. You think, "How did she get that scratch on her face? Wasn't she just born?" Of course, the scratch always shows up the day you have professional photos scheduled.

- 4-6 bottles (4 and 8 ounce size) and a variety of nipples. Even if you are planning on strict breastfeeding, there may be times when you express your milk and if you have a bottle on hand your partner can feed the baby. There are two kinds, regular ones that are either plastic or glass, and those with disposable, pre-sterilized liners. The plastic ones have to be BPA-free. You may have to try several nipples to see which ones your baby prefers. Avoid bottles in weird shapes because they are difficult to clean.

- 2 nursing bras (if nursing). Nursing bras are special bras that unclip from the top and fold down. I highly recommend Bravado nursing bras. They are extremely comfortable and they have great fabrics and colors. It's important to avoid underwire because they can compress the milk ducts and cause blocked ducts. Try Motherhood stores as well.

- Breast pads (if nursing). Buy soft cotton ones (several layers thick) that you can throw in the washer and dryer. When you breastfeed, milk comes out of both breasts at first and then the breast that the baby is not feeding from stops, so you need pads tucked into your bra to soak up any leaks. You also leak milk until your milk gets established. They make plastic backed breast pads that are waterproof, but only wear them occasionally, such as if you are going out to a party, because if you wear them all the time your breasts won't breathe and you can develop thrush.

- Breast pump (if nursing). There is a more detailed summary of breast pumps later I the book. For a manual pump, I recommend the Avent Pump. For an electric pump, I can recommend the Purely Yours by Ameda. I have owned, and used, both of these. Do not go out and buy one right away. Often you can rent one from your local pharmacy if you only need it for a few weeks.

- 6 bibs - the ones that fasten with velcro around the baby's neck are better than the ones that tie because as your baby's hair gets longer, you will find that sometimes you actually tie their hair when trying to tie a bib. And the bigger the bib, the better. The small ones hardly cover any of the baby's shirt. Bibs are not just for when you are feeding solids; they can catch burped up milk and catch drooling spit too.

- 10+ wash cloths - the more the better. Use these to wipe little hands, faces, etc. Baby washcloths are softer, thinner and smaller than "adult" washcloths.

- 4 bassinet sheets – obviously only if you have a bassinet! Make sure they are the right fit, then wash them and put them away.

- 3-4 crib sheets - if you have a crib. These are bigger than bassinet sheets.

- 2 crib blankets - I like the knitted ones that are "holey" because then I don't have to worry if my baby puts it over her face. Put it up to your face and see if you can breathe through it before you let your baby sleep with it.

- 6-8 snap t-shirts or onesies

- 4-6 lightweight sleepers

- 6-8 receiving blankets (you will use these for swaddling)

- 10 pairs of socks (These can also double as gloves)

- 2 sweaters

- Booties - Robeez are great. They are made of leather, adorable and they do not fall off. Moms and pediatricians recommend them.

- Baby Swing – I highly recommend that you get a swing. The battery operated ones are better than the wind up ones because the latter stop swinging after 30 minutes and that usually wakes up the baby. Either that or you go running over there in a panic to wind it up again, trip on the laundry on the floor and wake up the baby with your shrieking.

- Bouncy Chair – This is a little reclining fabric chair that you can safely leave your baby in while you are taking a shower, making dinner, etc. (Don't feel guilty if you don't get around to making dinner!) Get one that has a vibrating feature you can turn off and on.

- Crib or bassinet – If you buy a crib, make sure you can lower the side rail to put the baby in. I prefer a side rail that lowers with a foot mechanism rather than the ones that you have to use two hands to lower. Why? Because if someone takes the baby out without lowering the side (i.e. your husband reaches in and lifts baby out), later when you tiptoe into the room holding your sleeping baby only to realize that you cannot lower the side because you need two hands to do it, and therefore have to break your back to lower the baby in without waking her up, you will wish you had one that you can lower with your foot. Believe me. Also, if you buy a second hand crib, make sure it still passes safety standards.

- Breastfeeding pillow – I highly recommend that you get a breastfeeding pillow so that you can be as comfortable as possible while breastfeeding. You don't want to get the baby latched on perfectly, only to realize that you now have to hold him in an uncomfortable position until he's finished.

What you don't need

You might find these things on "must-have" lists, but I disagree:

- bottle brush - this is a round brush on a wire handle that you shove into the bottle to clean it out. I guess it could be handy, but I've never used one.

- nasal aspirator - these are usually blue in color, and they are used to extract mucous out of your baby's nose. Some people use them all the time when their kids have colds, and others say they should not be used at all unless by a doctor. I say, you certainly do not need to go out and buy one before the baby arrives home, but one day you may be in the drugstore and see one and think, "Yeah, maybe I'll pick one of those up today". Wait and see.

- alcohol wipes (for the umbilical cord). Now they are saying to just leave the cord alone. I never did anything to either of my kids' cords and everything turned out fine! Ask your doctor or midwife.

- baby brush and comb set. How much hair can the kid have? You will probably get this as a shower gift any way.

- hooded bath towels – You do not *need* one of these. Just use a regular towel; your baby will never know the difference. They are cute, and I'm glad I received one as a gift, but they're not really necessary.

- crib bumper - you are not supposed to use bumpers until your baby is one year old due to SIDS. You have to make sure that air can circulate effectively all around your baby when she's lying down.

- comforters – you can't use the thick types of comforters until your baby is much older and the risk of SIDS has lessened.

Setting Up Your Nursing Station

If you are planning on breastfeeding, you should have a special place set up so that you will always be comfortable and relaxed when breastfeeding.

It can be in the corner of your living room, in your bedroom, in your baby's room, or anywhere you like. Personally, I liked to watch TV when nursing because I wasn't coordinated enough to hold a book with one hand and it was *really boring* to sit and stare at the wall for 10 hours a day. (You really will be nursing 10 hours a day! But, believe me, it is worth it.)

Your nursing station should have a rocking chair or other comfortable chair. When you are just beginning to get accustomed to nursing, you might find that a Boppy (a type of nursing pillow – shaped like a semi circle) will help you.

Make sure that you are completely relaxed and you are not holding any tension in your arms or shoulders. At first, you will probably have to ask your partner to place a pillow under your arm or elsewhere to get it "just right". Do not make the mistake of nursing in an uncomfortable position! It can cause injuries that last a long time. I know what it's like, believe me, especially if you have a tough time getting her to latch on... sometimes you think, "I don't care if I have to hold my arm like this, at least she's finally latched on." However, if you get a pulled muscle, or a kink in your neck so severe that you can't carry your baby, you'll regret it. So make sure you are 100% comfortable when nursing. Check in with yourself and literally ask yourself, am I holding my arm up, am I holding my shoulder up? Am I totally relaxed?

You will also need a table within reach to hold essentials. Nursing makes you really thirsty so I recommend a water bottle with a straw; that worked great for me. On your table, you might also have: a hair elastic, some lip balm, a notepad and paper, a phone (with a headset – highly recommended so you don't get a kink in your neck!), hand cream, and lanolin nipple cream (personally, I only used this in the first few weeks, and some women never use it at all). Make your nursing station a nice, inviting space for yourself. After all, you will be spending a lot of time there.

Chapter 6: Your First Day Home

How exciting! Your baby is finally here and now you are ready to bring her home! The first things you will need are an outfit and a car seat.

The Outfit

When you go to the hospital, be sure to pack something soft and warm for your baby to wear. Those cute little jeans you have might be better for later. Remember, your baby just was naked in warm, soft water for nine months and you want to try to emulate that comfort level that she's used to.

Soft cotton pajamas (also called sleepers) are great, with an undershirt underneath and don't forget a hat as well. (Babies lose a lot of heat from their heads). After you place her in the car seat, place a blanket over her. You can't put a blanket under the car seat restraint. Ask your nurse to check to make sure your baby is buckled in her seat correctly. Many hospitals won't let you leave until the nurse checks your car seat.

The Car Seat

The most important aspect of buying a car seat is making sure that it is safe. Make sure that it meets safety standards, and that it is appropriate for your type of car. It's a good idea to visit your AAA office and see if they do car seat safety checks – 90% of car seats are NOT installed, or used, properly!

There are safety concerns associated with buying a secondhand car seat, such as whether or not the car seat has been involved in a car accident and the age of the car seat. Check and see if the car seat has an expiry date stamped on the bottom.

Talk to Your Baby

Let your baby know what's going on. Tell her that you are going to take her home now. Scientists don't really know exactly when babies begin to understand us, so why not start talking to her right away?

Use a soft, gentle voice and encourage your partner to talk to your baby as well. She has already heard your voices for months and it will make her feel safe to hear you speaking to her.

According to the U.S. Department of Education, it is very important to talk to your baby. You may wonder how much of what you say is understood by your baby. But don't worry. When you talk, your baby is listening.

At first it may seem weird (I know!) but you'll get used to it very quickly. When you talk to your baby, use simple words and phrases. You should speak clearly. You can get your baby's attention by widening your eyes and mouth. You can also change the pitch and tone of your voice. These are your baby's first lessons in communicating.

Here are some tips for talking to your baby (from the US Department of Education):

- Look at your baby's eyes while you are talking to her.

- Call your baby by her name.

- Keep your talk simple. Say "sweet baby", "my sweetheart", "darling", "beautiful". Use the words "mommy" and "daddy" when you talk to her.

- Watch for your baby's expressions and listen to her sounds. Make these same sounds and facial expressions back to her.

- Add gestures to your talk. Say "wave bye-bye to daddy" as you wave to daddy.

- Ask your baby questions. "Would Maria like to have her milk now?" "Does Maria want to go outside?" Ask the questions even though she can't answer.

- Talk about what you are doing. As you dress, bathe and change your baby, talk about what you're doing.

- Read to your baby. Babies love nursery rhymes and poems. I must admit, sometimes I would just read my current novel out loud to Hana.

- Don't forget about your public library. You'll be amazed at how many cool baby books there are there.

- How about singing to your baby? It's important while she begins to learn language skills. Don't worry about your singing abilities – she will love your singing voice, even if you don't!

- Watch for signals from your baby when you are talking to her. If she is smiling and keeping eye contact, she is saying she wants you to keep on talking. If she keeps looking away, this means she is tired and wants a break.

In the car on the way home

Nurse your baby right before you leave the hospital, because by the time you really leave, it will be about an hour later! (You should get used to being late all the time now, it's OK, really, you're parents now.)

I like to suggest that you sit beside your baby in the backseat of the car, so that she can see you, hear you and smell you. Of course, be sure to wear your seatbelt.

If you're sitting beside her, you can calm her down if she gets fussy by placing your hand on her tummy, or stroking her head. She will probably fall asleep.

Never, ever take her out of her car seat while the car is moving. If you have a long drive and you need to nurse on the way home, pull over to a safe spot and stop the car.

On your way home, take a moment to think about the other women you see walking down the street with their children. They are mothers, and suddenly now you are too! They would walk to the end of the earth for their children. They would do anything to protect them, or help them. You too will soon know how this feels.

CB

"Most of all the other beautiful things in life come by twos and threes, by dozens and hundreds. Plenty of roses, stars, sunsets, rainbows, brothers and sisters, aunts and cousins, comrades and friends - but only one **mother** *in the whole world. "*

~Kate Douglas Wiggin

Chapter 7: Arriving Home

Once you arrive home, introduce your baby to the house and show her around a little. (However, if she's asleep, it can wait until later.) You can say, "This is where we hang our coats, and this is where we put our shoes..."

You can show your baby her room and say, "This is *your* room! Look at your nice crib and your little clothes we have all ready for you..." You can say, "Mommy and daddy are so happy that you are finally here, and we can't wait to spend time with you, and play with you and cuddle with you..."

Your baby will probably be ready to nurse again by the time you get home. You should take off any extra layers you have on her and get yourself settled with a drink like tea or water.

You can see why I recommended that you set up your nursing station before your baby arrives. You don't want to walk in the door with your new baby and then have to think about where might be a comfortable place to nurse, because by the time you figure it out, she'll probably be hysterically crying.

So when you get home, show her around and then get ready to feed her. Change her diaper first and then feed her. I always recommend that you change your baby's diaper before nursing, although some people suggest changing baby between breasts. I once heard that a husband said, "Change the baby between breasts? Isn't that a little unhygienic?" What they mean is feed baby on one breast, change her diaper (which will wake her up) and then feed her on the other breast.

If your baby falls asleep while breastfeeding, you have to wake her up so she can finish eating. It seems cruel, but you really must wake her up, otherwise you will have her attached to your breast for 24 hours a day. You will also have problems with her getting too much foremilk and not enough hindmilk. Take my word for it, you have to wake her up if she falls asleep. There's more information in the Breastfeeding section.

If you are bottle feeding, feed your baby half the recommended amount, burp her and change her diaper and then feed her the other half.

Safety First

Keep in mind that your baby will probably sleep a lot. It doesn't matter where she sleeps as long as you keep her safe.

If she falls asleep in her car seat, you can leave her in it, but bring her into whatever room you're in so you can keep an eye on her. It's hard to believe, but there has been at least one case where a car seat in which a baby was sleeping flipped over and the baby died.

Babies can also overheat when they're covered in blankets in their car seat so be careful of that too.

When Hana was a baby she would only nap in her baby swing and my mom always said that she thought it was bad for her. My mom said that babies should sleep flat on their back. I tried everything else and the only thing that worked was the baby swing. I was worried about what my mom was saying. I felt like I must be a failure if I couldn't get my daughter to nap in her crib like a "normal" baby.

Finally one day I called the Newborn Hotline (a phone number that connects you with a nurse) and asked the nurse about Hana napping in the baby swing, and she said, "Congratulations on finding a way to get your baby to nap! Whatever you are doing, keep doing it."

Trust your instincts. And believe in your parenting skills. Some days it seems like everyone is criticizing you, but you are your baby's mother, and you really do know best.

It's kind of funny because the swing has a label on it that states, "Do not leave baby unattended" and I always felt a bit perplexed by it. I thought, "Do I have to sit here staring at her?" Eventually I put her swing outside my bedroom door and then I could take a nap and I would sleep until Hana woke up and cried.

When your baby is in her crib or bassinet, make sure that there are NO toys, NO pillows, NO bumper pads, NO quilts, absolutely NOTHING in the crib with her, except one "holey" blanket that she is swaddled in.

"This too shall pass"

No matter what you are going through with your child – whether she is waking up seven times a night, every night, or she doesn't like taking a bath, or she freaks out over the vacuum cleaner – remind yourself that it's just a phase. Once the phase is over (and it *will* end eventually) you will look back and think, "Oh, I thought that would never end…" but it always does. As you are rocking your baby for hours, or pacing in the hallway, just repeat to yourself, "This too shall pass."

Actually, it passes way too fast!

Chapter 8: Giving Your Baby a Bath

It can be intimidating bathing infants the first few times. They seem so fragile and wiggly, not to mention slippery! But take heart! Follow these easy steps and you'll soon be teaching all your friends about bathing newborn babies like an experienced maternity nurse.

Lucky for me, all my babies have always enjoyed their bath time. When Alexa was about 4 months old she started to cry at bath time, but I soon realized that she was crying when I took her out of the bath because she loved it so much!

Bathing your new baby is really a lot of fun.

Pre-planning is all it takes to ensure that your baby's bath runs smoothly. It's funny because the bath itself only takes a couple of minutes, but getting it ready and finding the right time to do it can seem like the whole day has gone by.

Getting Ready for the bath

Many people recommend warming up the room where you are bathing your baby. I personally have never done this because I always bathe my babies in the kitchen and I don't have a heater in there. What am I going to do - turn on the oven? Just kidding! Needless to say, my babies are alive and well and not the least bit chilled today.

Supplies

Next, make sure you have all your supplies ready and within reach. Once the baby is undressed, it's too late. You have to keep your hands on her the whole time and can't be reaching for things or she will try to hurtle herself off the counter. Here's what I recommend:

- Fill baby bath or kitchen sink with lukewarm water (I like to fold a towel and lay it on the bottom of the sink so it is cushy on your baby's bottom, and she won't slip around)
- Mild soap if desired
- Two washcloths (but once you're a pro I bet you only use one, like me!)
- A towel to lay baby on
- A towel for drying off
- 2 Fresh diapers (you never know when 'the big one' will come rushing out and ruin that clean diaper! Suddenly you are covered in you-know-what and you have

no other diaper within reach - better bathe her all over again! Yes, I am speaking from experience here.)

- Clean clothes

Tip: You can put the towels and clothes in the dryer beforehand to make them nice and warm for your baby.

You may choose to play music during the bath. Some people say that you should play music when bathing babies. But I think this is a great time for baby to be able to look into your eyes and hear your comforting words. Also, like Tracy Hogg recommends in her book Secrets of the Baby Whisperer be sure to treat your baby with respect and tell her what you are doing. You wouldn't want someone to plunge you into a bath without telling you what's going on, would you?

Say, "Hi sweetie, mommy's here. I know you're going to love this. Mommy is going to give you a bath now. You like your bath, don't you? It's nice and warm, isn't it sweetheart? Can you feel the nice water on your skin?"

Start the bath

You can keep your baby dressed so she stays warm while you wash her face and hair. Lay her on the countertop (this is why I like giving a bath in the kitchen because I like to use the counter beside the sink).

Eyes: Put a little bit of water on the washcloth. Wipe baby's eyelid from the inside corner to the outside corner. Use a clean corner of the washcloth for the other eye.

Face and neck: Use the same washcloth to gently clean baby's face with water only. Don't forget behind the ears (no need to get into the ears). Lift the chin gently to wash under the neck folds (it can get smelly in there!).

Hair: Holding baby's head and neck steady over the edge of the sink, squeeze a little warm water from a washcloth onto baby's head. Next, squeeze a tiny bit of shampoo (if using) on and lather. Rinse with the wet washcloth and dry.

Into the bath: Now you are ready to undress your baby and gently place her in the bath. Test the temperature of the water by dipping your elbow into it. You can also buy bath thermometers in cute shapes but don't get too overly anxious about it. Remember that your common sense is sound. Clean her chest, stomach and arms with the washcloth. The folds of her armpits can also get stinky so make sure you get in there too. You do not have to use soap if you don't want to - plain water is fine. If you use a mild soap, squeeze a little bit onto the wet washcloth and follow with a water-only washcloth to rinse.

Then carefully hold your baby in a sitting position, leaning her against one forearm or roll onto her stomach, while you clean her back. Your whole hand can lie across her chest, with your thumb pretty much under her armpit and around to her back.

Careful, they're slippery!

Follow any instructions from your doctor for care of the umbilical cord. When I had my first baby, the advice of the day was to use alcohol, but I never got around to it. Once my second baby came along, the advice of the day was not to do anything with the cord. See? Mothers do know best.

Next, move on down to her legs and feet with the warm washcloth. If using soap, rinse well with the water-only cloth, getting in all the cute little creases of fat. Use a new washcloth to clean the genitals. For girls, remember to clean from front to back. It is not necessary to clean inside the labia every time, just now and then. The mucus in between a girl's labia is normal and does not have to be completely removed in order to be "clean". If you have a boy, and you have chosen to circumcise him, follow your pediatrician's (or doctor's) recommendations for caring for circumcisions.

One other thing: I do use soap on baby's feet because people like to kiss their feet all the time! Also, as baby gets older, she will start to put her feet in her mouth so it's good for them to be squeaky clean.

Lastly, gently lift baby out of the bath and lay her on the towel you have placed on the counter. You may choose to use powder or lotion at this time, or not. My first daughter had extremely sensitive skin so I couldn't use any lotions on her at all. But my second and third babies had no problems, so I liked to use lotion that makes them smell heavenly. Put on your baby's diaper, dress her, and you're done. Now your baby is sweet-smelling once again. The more you do it, the more comfortable you will feel at it.

There you have it. That's all there is to it. You are now an expert at bathing newborn babies! Have fun!

Chapter 9: For Crying Out Loud!

All newborn babies **need to cry as a means of communication**. That's why it is so important to pick them up when they are crying; it is not until much later that you can let a baby "cry it out" (if you choose). You simply cannot spoil a new baby by paying attention to them every time they cry.

It has been proven that when parents respond right away to their baby's crying, the baby learns to find other ways to express herself.

According to statistics, newborn babies cry on average between 1 to 5 hours out of every 24. (I think Hana cried more than ten hours a day!)

While you cannot influence your baby's innate predisposition to crying, you can do something about how long she cries.

The 5 Causes of Crying:

There are five common reasons for babies to cry.

#1 Hunger

This is the most common cause. It is normal for babies to nurse every two to three hours, and that is counting from the beginning of the feed, not the end.

Sometimes you feel like it must not be hunger that's bothering your baby because you feel like you just finished feeding her! But check your watch; it may have been two hours since you started. Your baby could be having a growth spurt when she's nursing more frequently.

You can tell if she's hungry if you are holding her in your arms and she is "rooting", that is, if she is craning her head around towards your chest. She may also be sucking on her hand.

It is not recommended to nurse more often than every two hours, because your body needs enough time to actually make the milk. I found that, initially, Hana was sometimes nursing every hour and a half, but after seeing a doctor who specialized in breastfeeding, I learned that she was only getting foremilk during each feed and was not nursing long enough to get the rich, satisfying hindmilk. Getting too much foremilk was causing gas and making her cry.

While breastfeeding is one of the most natural things in the world, as I mentioned before, I would really recommend that if you want to be successful, that you read a little bit on it. I have listed some excellent books in the Resources section.

#2 Dirty diaper

Even if you just changed her diaper, check it again. Some babies are very sensitive to a wet bottom and this can really set them off.

#3 Gas

You should try to get a good burp out of your baby after (or during) every feed. When babies curl their legs up to their tummy and look as if they're in pain, they probably have gas.

One thing you can try to alleviate gas is a product called **Gripe Water**. I found that Woodward's brand is the best. Sometimes babies get muscle spasms and excess acid created when air bubbles form in baby's tummy. If the baby's stomach is full of air bubbles, her muscles don't relax, causing cramps. Woodward's Gripe Water contains Oil of Dill herb and Sodium Bicarbonate and brings relief to some babies. Most people I know swear by it. Dill Seed Oil warms and relaxes the tummy, breaking down trapped air bubbles. Sodium Bicarbonate neutralizes acid in the baby's tummy. Note: You cannot give it to babies under one month old.

Funny Story: When my friend's baby was about six weeks old, she was exasperated one night with her baby's discomfort and shouted at her husband, "Go get some gripe water!" and off he dutifully went to the store. It seemed like he was gone forever. Finally, he returned and said, "They didn't have any grape water buy I got grape juice and thought we could mix it with water??"

#4 Lonely

Sometimes babies just want to be held and cuddled and want to feel safe.

#5 Tired or over stimulated

This one always confused me with Hana. I always thought it was so weird how difficult it was for us to get her to sleep when she was tired. Babies can get especially fussy at parties where everyone wants to hold the baby and they get passed around from person to person.

CB

"Always kiss your children goodnight, even if they are already asleep."

~Jackson Browne

Crying Checklist

So, when your baby cries, ask yourself:

#1. Is it her diaper?

Check it. If baby stops crying, great! You knew exactly what to do.

#2. Is she hungry?

If you have fed her within the last two hours, I would try to wait a bit. Don't always assume it's hunger (as soon as baby makes a peep, dads always say, "I think she's hungry"... just wait, you'll see what I mean!).

#3. Does she need to burp?

There are four ways to burp your baby:

1. Hold baby upright with her tummy on your chest area and baby's head looking over your shoulder. Gently rub her back from the bottom to the top, up and down her back.

2. Same position, but try patting. Some people do not recommend this method, but I always found that it worked well.

3. Lie baby facedown across your lap and pat or rub her back.

4. This one is funny, but it always worked for me. If I couldn't get a burp out of my baby when she was upright, I would slowly lower her down until she was lying flat on her back on my lap, then quickly put

her up on my shoulder again. It would basically force the burp up and out of her. Sometimes babies barf when you do this so be forewarned!

If she hasn't burped after five minutes or so, give it a rest and try again later.

#4. Does she need a change of scene?

Bring her into the kitchen to see what you're doing. Talk to her and tell her what's going on around the house. If she's been in her bouncy chair for a while, maybe she wants to lie down flat. Or maybe she just wants to be cuddled.

#5. Is she tired?

Is your baby rubbing her eyes? Are her eyes red? My babies always had red eyes when they're tired. You will get to be such an expert that you only need to look at your babies eyes and you'll know if she's tired. It can be surprising; sometimes they need to nap really soon after they wake up.

#6. Does she need to suck?

Give her a soother or let her suck on your finger. (See The Pacifier Debate later in this book.)

Make sure your pinky (smallest) finger is <u>clean</u> and your nail is cut short, then insert it upside down into her mouth. In other words, your fingernail should be on her tongue, and the soft part of your finger should be touching the roof of her mouth.

You'd be surprised how hard she can suck!

Chapter 10: Fifteen Surefire Ways to Calm Crying

Ok, let's say that you have checked all of the above and she is still crying; try one of these 15 Surefire Way to Calm Crying. I swear to you, they ALL work! You will be so happy to have these techniques you're going to want to kiss me!

1. Tour Guide

Hold your baby in an upright position with her head looking over your shoulder. Show her pictures and plants around the room. Describe them to her, like, "Look Sarah, here is a plant with long skinny leaves. We don't know what kind it is, but we call him Spike. And over here is a picture of Grandma. She used to have long hair. Now she has short hair, doesn't she?" Continue distracting her by showing her all around the room until she's calm.

2. Bobbing for baby

Hold your baby and while standing, bend at your knees repeatedly so you are gently bobbing up and down. It may help to say, "Shh shh shh" right into her ear as well. Hold your hand on the back of her head firmly – do not shake her. The rhythmic bobbing, over and over, may drive you nuts but it is soothing for babies.

3. Change artist

Change position. Sometimes baby just doesn't like the way you're holding her. If she's sideways (cradle hold) change her to upright on your shoulder. It works.

4. White Noise

Hold baby tightly in your arms. Go into the bathroom, turn off the light and turn on the bathroom fan. Stand perfectly still, holding her tightly against you – obviously not too tight! Give it a minute or two. If being still doesn't work, try swaying a little back and forth.

5. Hum

Get your partner to remove his shirt and lie semi-reclined on your bed or couch. Remove baby's shirt also and have dad hold baby skin-to-skin, and cover them both with a blanket. Dad holds baby with her head on his chest and dad hums. It doesn't matter if you hum tunes, or hum randomly, just hum. She will love to hear and feel dad's humming. Try stroking baby's back or head as well.

6. Five S's (or 4 S's and one J)

Dr. Harvey Karp's method (see Resources) is fantastic. Start by swaddling your baby really tight. Put a soother in her mouth and pick her up, having her lie on her side, with her tummy facing your tummy. Jiggle her a bit, being careful not to shake her. (This is the J for jiggle, instead of S for shake). Now say SHHH SHHHH SHHHH quite loudly in her ear, over and over. She'll be calm in no time. It really works!

7. Couch potato

Let her watch TV. It works! We used to put on the Country Music Channel and it totally distracted Hana.

8. Touchy Feely

Give her a baby massage. Gentle, soothing stroking of her arms and legs can really calm a baby. Some babies like this, and some don't. You'll know right away if she likes it or not!

9. Water Baby

Give her a nice warm bath. Some babies find this very relaxing.

10. Rock on

Turn down the lights and put on soft music. Hold your baby and dance around the room. My father-in-law said he did this with James to the Beatles for hours and hours!

11. Hold tight

Swaddle your baby (see How to Swaddle Your Baby) and lie down with her beside you in bed. Hold her really close to you, tummy to tummy.

If you are lying on your right side, put your right arm up above your shoulder and around baby's head, with your right hand on her back or torso. Your left arm should be on her legs or back as well. Put your mouth on baby's forehead or head and say, "Shhhhhh" over and over in kind of a lulling, "white noise" kind of way. Your lips will literally be touching her head so she can feel your breath.

Do it louder than baby's cry so she can hear you.

I remember one time I did this with Alexa when she was about two weeks old. She was really upset and I couldn't seem to settle her and get her to sleep. Eventually the "sussshing" worked because we both fell sound asleep and when I woke up her forehead was wet from my saliva!

12. Let's swing!

Try using a baby swing. While most makes say that you can't use them until a baby is 6 weeks old, I used it anyways. Make sure baby is belted in properly.

13. Swing it more!

Another option (which was one of the only things that worked with Hana) is to put the baby swing in your kitchen, turn on the fan over the stove, and turn out the lights.

14. Wanna go for a ride?

Go out for a car ride. A lot of people swear by this.

15. Forget it

Sometimes your baby just wants to be left alone. Place her, screaming, in her crib or bassinet and walk away. This is a great time to close the door, walk down the hallway, turn on the shower and have a nice long scrub, especially if you're on your last nerve. It won't hurt her to cry for ten minutes. Sometimes by the time you get out of the shower, she is fast asleep.

Chapter 11: The Pacifier Debate

Way before babies can do much else, they can suck. And it is an important means of self-soothing for them. They are either going to suck their mother's breast, suck their fingers, or suck a pacifier.

I remember when Hana was only a few days old, and I was feeling like a human pacifier because she was nursing around the clock, James and I looked at each other bleary-eyed at about 3am and said, "What's the controversy about pacifiers again? Why shouldn't we let her have one?" And we couldn't think of what it was, so we gave her one and she started sucking madly and suddenly fell sound asleep. From then on, it really helped her get to sleep.

Some parents say that they are not going to give their next child a pacifier while others swear they are going to get their next baby on a pacifier no matter what.

Of course the choice is up to you. For me, personally, I am all for it!

Some of the benefits of pacifiers

- They can help your baby self soothe to sleep

- They can help baby get back to sleep in the middle of the night

- They can help distract the baby, for example while you are getting a bottle ready or finding a place to nurse if you are out

Some of the disadvantages of pacifiers

- They may cause your baby to have "nipple confusion". What this means is that her tongue moves differently with a pacifier, breast and bottle and some people say that it could interfere with breastfeeding

- Long term use can cause dental problems

- It can be hard to get rid of

If you do use a pacifier, make sure you wash it every day with hot soapy water and rinse well because the soapy water can get inside. And if I were you, I'd buy several of exactly the same kind in case you lose one!

Tip: When your baby is older, you might find that you have to go into her room at night to put the pacifier back in her mouth. Here's a tip that my aunt Marg gave me. Put 5 or 6 of the exact same pacifiers in her crib! She will be able to reach around and find one and pop it back into her mouth, saving you countless trips to her crib.

Getting Rid of the Pacifier

I know you may be thinking, "I don't want a 4 year old sucking on a pacifier." Yes, I agree that sometimes it goes on a bit too long and you might be wondering how you will ever get rid of it. Here is something that we did and it worked great! We invented the Soother Fairy. When our kids were ready (or somewhat ready) we explained to them that soothers are for little babies and our big girl didn't need it anymore and pretty soon the Soother Fairy was going to come and bring them a present! We would talk about it for a few days until our kids fully understood what was happening. Then we would get a brown paper bag and decorate it, again mentioning that this was for the Soother Fairy. Then we would gather up all the soothers in the house and place them in the bag. Before bed that night, we set the bag on the front steps for the Soother Fairy. The next morning, all the soothers in the bag were gone and in their place was a brand new stuffie!

It worked every time.

03

"It's not only children who grow. Parents do too. As much as we watch to see what our children do with their lives, they are watching us to see what we do with ours. I can't tell my children to reach for the sun. All I can do is reach for it myself."

~Joyce Maynard

Chapter 12: Sleep

Newborns sleep an average of 16 hours a day. Some sleep as few as 10.5 hours and some as much as 20 hours. Babies regulate their need for sleep and usually nap for 2 to 4 hours at a time.

The first thing you need to know about a new baby is that you will become obsessed with getting them to sleep! They do not know the difference between day and night (until you teach them) and you'll find that on average, they wake up 2 to 3 times a night. This is normal. Don't listen to the women who tell you their babies sleep all night long from 6 weeks old – it'll make you crazy with envy.

The reason babies sleep so much is that their neurological systems grow much faster when they are sleeping and, obviously, they have a lot more growing to do than adults.

Most newborn babies fall asleep easily, and many new parents are surprised that it can be quite a challenge keeping their baby awake for feedings. When they get to be a few weeks old, they cry when they're tired and it can be challenging getting them to sleep.

Your baby is used to being rocked to sleep since this is how she felt when she was in the womb.

Therefore, you will probably find that any type of movement will help your baby fall asleep.

Many of the 15 techniques discussed in "15 Surefire Way to Calm Crying", will help your baby fall asleep in addition to calming them.

The Ten Commandments of Sleep:

1.) Swaddle tightly. Young babies are used to being in a cramped position and they don't like to have their arms and legs flailing around.

2.) Keep a calm atmosphere. Keep light and noise down to a minimum.

3.) Or, turn on the vacuum cleaner. (If this works for your baby, make a recording and play the recording, otherwise you will wear out your vacuum and your carpet!). One time, when my baby niece was about 8 or 9 weeks old, we were over at their house for dinner. After dinner, my sister and brother-in-law were in her bedroom, trying and trying to calm her down. She was just bawling and bawling inconsolably. I didn't want to butt in, but I wanted to help, so I quietly snuck into the room and gently asked Chris to go and get the hairdryer. He looked at me like I was nuts, but he did it. I plugged it in, turned it on low in the corner of the room, and within ONE minute, their baby was sound asleep!

4.) Loud hard rock music sometimes works too! (At least you can drown out the crying and give yourself a break!)

5.) Driving in the car.

6.) Strapping your baby in her car seat and placing it on the clothes dryer while it's running. (Do not leave her unattended; she could fall off!)

7.) Give her a soother or let her suck on your clean pinky finger, with your fingernail facing down toward her tongue.

8.) Hold baby close to you, either rocking in chair or keeping still, and gently stroke her eyebrow, over and over again, very slowly. Go from the inside edge to the outside edge. (I know it sounds ridiculous, but it works! My now 8 year old still likes it.)

9.) Go for a walk with baby in her stroller or a sling or a snugglie.

10.) Sing or hum. Don't worry if you think you can't sing; your baby will love the sound of your voice.

Why Babies Wake Up

Generally babies wake up because they are hungry or uncomfortable. Their little tummies are so small they burn through their last feeding quickly and they need to eat again. That's why they can sleep for longer periods as they get older because as they grow they can store more food.

They are also more likely to dirty their diaper when sleeping when they're very young.

You may notice that sometimes they wake themselves up with their own startle reflex. They fling their arms out to the side and it wakes them up. Swaddling your baby with her arms tucked in will prevent this.

ය

"Your children need your presence more than your presents."

~Jesse Jackson

How to put your baby down when she's asleep (and keep her that way)

This used to drive me crazy. I would spend two or three hours calming Hana and finally get her to sleep and then try to put her in her crib and she'd wake up and I'd have to do it all over again.

Here are some things you can try:

1.) Place a hot water bottle in her crib and cover it with the blanket she will use. Just before you put her in the crib, have your partner take out the hot water bottle. **Do not** put your baby in the crib with the hot water bottle (it's a suffocation hazard). Slowly lower your sleeping baby into the warm crib.

2.) Rock your baby in your arms and continue rocking gently as you lower her into the crib. Sometimes what they are afraid of is the feeling of falling through open space. Place your baby in the crib and keep your arms around her for a moment. Then carefully withdraw your arms. This is what Dr. Sears recommends (see Resources).

3.) Place your sleeping baby in her crib and then gently jiggle the crib a bit to trick her into thinking that she's still being rocked in your arms.

4.) Get one of those gadgets that make heartbeat noises and white noise and place it near her crib. You can get these at most drugstores or online.

5.) Place mom's t-shirt in her crib so she can smell her mom's scent. Remove the shirt once you know she's asleep.

6.) Play soft music in her room.

ɔ

"The quickest way for a parent to get a child's attention is to sit down and look comfortable."

~Lane Olinghouse

How to Swaddle

I highly recommend swaddling your baby. helps keep them calm and almost all babies LOVE being swaddled.

- Spread out a receiving blanket in a diamond shape and fold the top corner down.

- Lay your baby on top, with her neck at the fold.

- Take the point on the left and fold it across her body, holding her arm straight at her side, and tuck the blanket tightly under her.

- Fold the bottom corner up to her tummy. If it's too long, you can fold it in half.

- Now fold the right side over across her body and wrap it snugly under her, tucking it in.

- Your baby's legs can still move, but her arms are held still.

Most babies will calm down considerably when swaddled like a little sausage.

Chapter 13: All About Breastfeeding

Benefits

The decision to breastfeed or not is a personal one that only you can make. I have had both a great experience and a difficult experience breastfeeding my kids. It seems strange to say, but now I actually *miss* breastfeeding!

Breast milk is one of the greatest gifts you can give your child.

Extensive research has shown that breast milk offers the absolute perfect nutrition for your baby as well as significant immunological benefits as well. In addition, consider the following proven facts:

- Breastfed babies have increased protection against diabetes, allergies and meningitis.

- Breast milk also helps protect babies from ear infections, diarrhea, and colds and may help protect babies from S.I.D.S.

- The composition of breast milk changes as your baby grows and her nutritional needs change.

- When breastfed babies do get sick, studies show that they require hospitalization less frequently than formula-fed babies.

- Breastfeeding is more convenient, especially when you're on the go. There are no bottles to sterilize and no formula to refrigerate.

- Breastfeeding can save a family about $1200 a year.

- Women who breastfeed have a lesser chance of ovarian cancer and breast cancer. In fact, breast cancer affects women who have not breastfed to such a limited degree that it used to be called "the nuns' disease".

- Breastfeeding can also help you lose weight. Breastfeeding exclusively every day is the equivalent to riding a bicycle uphill for an hour a day or swimming 100 lengths in a pool.

- Lastly, breastfeeding is the *normal* way to feed a baby. It is not weird, or creepy, "personal", private, or embarrassing. It is totally normal.

My experience breast feeding Hana

Although I was 100% committed to breastfeeding Hana, I had tremendous difficulty, which I had not expected at all.

I kept getting blocked milk ducts (15 times!), a condition that is very painful.

She latched on poorly, and although I went to breast feeding clinics and doctors who specialized in breast feeding, nothing seemed to help.

Three good sources for breast feeding information are: www.askdrsears.com, www.lalecheleague.org and the many Dr. Newmann articles on www.breastfeedinginc.ca.

I hated breast feeding. I dreaded it because it hurt every time. I tried to get help and I felt so guilty. One day I was out for coffee with three other moms with young babies and I asked them. "Do you actually like breast feeding? I hate it." And they looked at me totally shocked. They all said they kind of liked it. I said, "I think I must be missing something." I think what it really was that I never got a good latch and I was always in pain, because of the blocked milk ducts. So I was totally tense.

I finally went to my doctor when Hana was 5 months old and said, "ARRGJGHJGH!! I can't do this anymore! I HATE breast feeding!!" My doctor very calmly replied, "You've done a fantastic job breastfeeding for five months. Go ahead and stop."

I was so relieved. I weaned Hana and started her on formula.

I was feeling better physically, but Hana's discomfort, crying and eczema persisted. She was still covered in eczema from head to toe and she would scratch at it and bleed. She had bloody sores all over her skin. To be honest, she looked disgusting.

When Hana was eight months old, my brother's wife called me and said, "Oh Suzanne, I can't believe I just thought of this. When Zachery was a baby, you were living overseas so you didn't know about the terrible eczema he had. When I switched him to 'lactose-free' formula, it cleared up."

Well, I felt like I had been told I had won the lottery! I had asked various doctors if her problems could have been caused by lactose intolerance and they all said that eczema is not caused by diet and that babies cannot be allergic to their mother's milk. (Ha!)

That is when the great transformation took place! Hana started on "Lactose-free" formula, the eczema cleared up within a week, and she started going to sleep at 8:00 pm and sleeping straight through until 8:00 am. Ahhh!!! Can you imagine how my life changed? I was so happy to finally have sleep, I was walking around with a permanent grin on my face.

In short, she became an easy, happy baby.

My experience with our second baby, Alexa, was completely different. From the get-go, she latched on perfectly and breast feeding was a fantastic experience that lasted for 12 months. She never even had a drop of formula.

When I nursed Alexa, I felt a very relaxed feeling rush over me and I felt totally content and peaceful. I never once had that feeling while breastfeeding Hana.

It just goes to show you, again, that every pregnancy and every baby is so very different.

Give your baby 40 days

I say you should give yourself and your baby 40 days. That's not too much to ask, is it?

If breastfeeding isn't working out after 40 days, and you've tried your very best, (i.e. you've gone to a breastfeeding clinic for help, you've called La Leche league for help, you've asked your doctor, midwife or public health nurse for help), then switch to formula.

And don't feel guilty! Remember, you've given your baby forty days of the very best nutrition possible.

Breastfeeding Tips

Establishing a good milk supply

- Frequent feedings: Your newborn baby should nurse 8 to 12 times in 24 hours. The amount of milk you produce is directly related to the amount of stimulation your breasts receive. Breastfeeding time should not be limited, and both breasts should be used at each feeding, alternating starting sides. If your baby has trouble latching on by day three, get help.

- Drink plenty of fluids: Nursing mothers need to drink a lot. If you remember to drink something every time you nurse your baby, you will stay hydrated. You'll know if you're drinking enough when you go to the bathroom; your urine should be pale and clear, not yellow.

- Rest when the baby rests: It is very important for new moms to rest. Ideally you should sleep when the baby sleeps for at least the first six weeks. With my second baby, I napped every afternoon with her (my older daughter was in daycare) for several months. It was heaven!

- Eat a balanced diet: You need to eat a nutritious diet while breastfeeding, just as you did while pregnant. Take care not to miss meals. You can make easy-to-eat meals the night before and put them in the fridge.

- Relax during feedings: Breastfeeding goes better if you are comfortable and relaxed during feedings. If your baby has trouble latching on by day 3, get help!

Positioning

Having the baby positioned properly for breast feeding is very important. Not only to avoid sore nipples but it also affects how much milk she'll get. Be sure to:

- Find a comfortable position, sitting up or lying down. Baby's tummy should be facing your tummy. You don't want her to have to turn her head around to latch on.

- Support your breast with your hand, thumb on top and fingers underneath.

- If your baby isn't interested, stimulate her by her lips with your finger or nipple. Then, with your baby's mouth WIDE open, quickly bring her to your breast. Don't try to bring your breast to the baby. Be patient and keep trying - this takes time for both of you to learn how to do this.

- Sometimes it can be *really* frustrating at the beginning. You feel like you have to try over and over and over again and you *just want to scream!!* Remember that you are not alone. Lots and lots of other women are going through the exact same thing as you are right now. You will get through it.

- At every feeding, be sure to get the nipple and a good portion of the areola well back into the baby's mouth.

- Imagine you are pointing your nipple slightly to the roof of your baby's mouth, not straight back to her throat. I learned this with my second child and this tip alone was the most helpful one I got.

- Your baby's lips should be flared out when latched properly. If one lip is tucked in, so to speak, you can pull it out a bit with your finger without having to re-latch.

- If you have to take your baby off your breast when you're breastfeeding (if someone arrives at your door, or you suddenly have to go to the bathroom), you must break the latch by slipping your finger in the corner of her mouth and breaking the suction. Otherwise it'll really hurt if you try to yank her off!

La Leche League is a volunteer group of women who know a lot about breastfeeding. Please don't think they are all crazy hippies. Sure, some of them may breastfeed for more years that you would choose, but they are VERY helpful and very kind. Sometimes all you need to completely solve your breast feeding problem is a tip from a mom who's been there. Go to http://www.lalecheleague.org to find help in your area.

Engorgement

Engorgement is defined as swollen, hard breasts, filled with milk. The best way to resolve it is to breastfeed.

Engorgement is what happens when your milk "comes in". It can be quite agonizing, but don't worry, it will pass. You'll be shocked at how huge your breasts will become!

When you give birth to your baby, your breasts are not yet filled with milk. Your milk comes in a few days later. With Hana mine didn't come in until Day Five! So for the first day (or few days) after birth, your baby is drinking colostrum, which is very, very good for her.

If your baby feeds frequently, engorgement will probably be relieved within 48 hours. To keep the areola soft so the baby can latch on to feed, try the following:

- Apply moist heat to the breast before feeding, expressing enough colostrum or milk to soften the areola.

- Stand in a hot shower with the water at your back, allowing the water to run over your shoulders and breasts. Express or pump milk while in the shower to soften the areola.

- You might need to limit the time the baby feeds on the first breast to make sure the baby will take the second breast during the feeding.

- Cabbage leaves work well to reduce engorgement. Take a regular, round, green cabbage and pull off the leaves and wash them. Using a sharp knife, cut out the stem in a V so the leaf stays whole with the stem cut out. Chill the leaves in the fridge. To relieve engorgement, place the leaf on your breast, not covering your nipple. I hope I'm explaining this well enough! In a nutshell, you wrap the cabbage leaf around your breast but use the space where the stem was to ensure that your nipple is not covered by the cabbage. You will feel immediate relief.

- Cold packs might relieve pain and swelling if used after feeding.

- If these measures do not relieve engorgement, call your midwife, doctor or public health nurse. In some places, you can also call the hospital where you gave birth.

ଔ

Remember my Mantra: This Too Shall Pass.

Make sure you get help if you need it. Ask for help and keep asking until you get it.

Sore Nipples

Sore nipples usually result from improper positioning. If it hurts, check your positioning and also follow these steps:

- Baby should feed first on the less sore side.

- Short, frequent feedings are better than long, infrequent feedings.

- Change feeding position to allow your baby's jaws to exert pressure on less sore areas.

- Remember to remove your baby from the breast by breaking the suction with your finger.

- Call your doctor or midwife if soreness continues or is severe!

- There are videos on Dr. Jack Newman's site at www.breastfeedinginc.ca. I highly recommend his advice.

Signs That Breastfeeding is Going Well

- Your new baby is feeding well 8 to 12 times every 24 hours.

- Your baby's urine is pale in color.

- Your baby wets at least six diapers every 24 hours after the third day.

- Your baby's poops are soft and mustard-colored by the end of the first week. How often she goes will vary, but she will probably poop frequently.

- If your baby gets back up to birth weight by 2 to 3 weeks of age and continues gaining, that's great! Remember that she will likely lose some weight at first so you need to keep an eye on her weight and make sure she's gaining.

- Let me re-state that: Almost ALL babies lose weight after birth, then begin to gain it back, so don't be alarmed. You DO need to keep an eye on it and make sure your baby is regaining the weight, but don't be scared. It's normal.

- If your baby is not having at least 6 wet diapers every 24 hours by day 5, call your doctor or midwife.

Chapter 14: The Truth about Formula

In an effort to make this book as complete as possible, I thought I should research whether or not there were any risks to giving your baby formula. I really didn't think there would be, but as I delved deeper and deeper into the research, I was shocked to learn that there are, in fact, many known and proven risks to giving your baby formula (which is also called "artificial infant feeding" in many research papers, in case you are interested in doing your own research).

Infant formula was invented by Henri Nestle in 1867 for rare cases where an otherwise healthy baby would have died because his mother could not breastfeed him for some reason or another. No one back then chose not to breastfeed.

Breast milk is rich in living white blood cells – formula has none. Breast milk is also rich in hormones, whereas the processing kills the hormones in formula, and they are not <u>human</u> anyway.

Breast milk has over 300 ingredients, while formula has only approximately 40.

One hundred and thirty oligosaccharides are present in human milk but not in formula. One company that I know of has added three oligosaccharides to its formula, which means that the other 127 are still missing.

Over the past many years, the recipe for formula has changed many times. They are not making it better, they are simply finding ways of making it "less worse", if you get my drift. The recipe for breast milk has not changed in thousands of years!

The fact is that formula does not meet the nutritional and immunity needs of infants. It is not, as the manufacturers claim, second best to breast milk, it is very, very inferior to breast milk. Most new mothers are clearly unaware of how important breast milk is for their baby. Everyone says, "Formula is just as good" and "My niece was formula fed and she turned out alright". The use of infant formula doubles the risk of infant death. This is something that no doctor will tell you, but it can be clearly seen through all the scientific research that has been undertaken.

Please understand that I am not trying to scare you. **Don't forget, I fed Hana formula too**! I had to because she has a terrible reaction to breastfeeding. It's rare, but it happens. The reason I am including this section is for women who are pregnant and are considering formula feeding because they think it'll just be easier and not as embarrassing as breast feeding. But the truth is that breast milk really is the greatest gift you can ever give your baby.

So if you need to skip this section, I understand. It is not my intention to make anyone feel guilty. Sometimes breastfeeding just doesn't work out. In two cases it worked for me and in one case it did not work for me. So I completely understand.

However, I think it's fascinating how, as a culture, we can take away something perfectly natural like breast feeding and make it dirty and brainwash everyone into thinking that formula is just as good. It's night and day.

The most recent US study on the risks of formula feeding demonstrates that formula fed infants have five times the risk of dying from S.I.D.S. than breastfed babies. Why would any mother knowingly put her baby at risk? It is because they do not know the facts. I'll say it again - I also formula fed my daughter Hana. She simply could not tolerate breast milk at all. So there was nothing I could do but give her formula.

I am not judging here, not at all! But if you want to formula feed, you should know the facts.

More than half the calories in breast milk come from fat, but since the formula manufacturers do not exactly know the complete makeup of breast milk, they add coconut oil and other oils to formula. According to John D. Benson, Ph.D., and Mark L. Masor, Ph.D. (who wrote in the March 1994 issue of Endocrine Regulations) "Human milk contains living cells, hormones, active enzymes, immunoglobulins and compounds with unique structures that cannot be replicated in infant formula." For reasons unclear to scientists, babies can absorb 100% of the iron in breast milk, but cannot absorb all the iron in formula.

Further, breast milk is ideally suited for the average infant, delivering all needed nutrients. It is a *species-specific* liquid containing unique substances such as living cells (e.g., macrophages), hormones, antibodies, active enzymes (which help digestion) and other proteins (e.g., immunoglobulins such as IgA) that cannot be artificially supplied to the infant.

Here's the most interesting fact of all which I think is **miraculous:** The breast milk changes depending on the time of day, and its fat content changes according to the time of the feeding episode ("fore" milk versus "hind" milk). Early milk (colostrum) contains proportionally greater amounts of protein and minerals and less fat than mature milk. These ratios reverse as the infant ages. Isn't that amazing? So the milk that your baby gets at one month old is different than the milk that she gets at 6 months old. How does your body know?

As I've mentioned, I gave my first daughter, Hana, formula from the age of five months up until she was one year old. In contrast, my second daughter never received a drop of formula, simply because breastfeeding was so successful and so easy that it wouldn't have made any sense for me to stop breastfeeding and give her formula. There is a striking difference between my two daughters' health; the older one, Hana, is sick far more often than

Alexa. There is no way of knowing if this is a direct result of formula feeding versus breast milk feeding, but I will always have my suspicions.

Ignoring the long-term effects of formula feeding for a moment, have you ever thought about the number of recalls on formula that occur from time to time? I never thought much about it until I had kids. Formula fed infants are at a high risk of exposure to life threatening bacterial contam-ination. Enterobacter sakazakii is a frequent contaminant in powdered formula and can cause sepsis and meningitis in newborns.

Between 1982 and 1994, there were 22 recalls of infant formula due to health and safety problems. The FDA classified 7 of these recalls as "life threatening". Products were recalled for such things as contamination by Salmonella, Enterobacter sakazakii, Klebsiella Pneumoniae, black plastic particles and bits of glass. You can go to the FDA's website and search "formula recalls" for more information.

Update: I just visited the above-mentioned site and found that since September 2010 there are currently 2,173 entries listed under Infant Formula Recall. One in particular had to be recalled because beetles and larvae were found in the finished product!

Interesting quote from the FDA's website: "FDA has determined that while the formula containing these beetles poses no long-term health problems, there is a possibility that infants who consume formula containing the beetles or their larvae could experience gastrointestinal discomfort and refusal to eat as a result of small insect parts irritating the GI tract. FDA is advising consumers who have recalled product not to feed it to their child."

The purpose of this section is absolutely NOT to *scare* mothers into breast feeding. I strongly believe that if more new mothers knew the risks associated with formula, they would be more willing to *try breastfeeding* and to *stick with it if it got difficult.* It is not my intention to make anyone feel guilty – remember, I formula fed my own baby!

Breastfeeding Support

I urge you to set up breastfeeding support before your baby's birth because the first 3 to 5 days are crucial to your success.

If you experience any problems, get help right away.

If your baby's latch is not right, it will be painful and it will not improve on its own; you must get help to sort it out.

There are many places to get breastfeeding help and advice, including:

- Your sister or friend who had a positive nursing experience.

- The hospital where you gave birth. Don't leave without a number you can call for help.

- Your family doctor. She can refer you to a clinic or lactation consultant, if she can't help you herself. If she's not supportive of breastfeeding, go somewhere else.

- La Leche League, the largest women's health organization in the world, has more than 3,000 breastfeeding support groups in 48 countries. Don't be intimidated by them. As I said before, contrary to what you might think, they're not judgmental hippy chicks – they are very nice women! They also offer telephone help. 1-800-La Leche is contacted more than 10,000 times a month. Check for La Leche League in the business section of your local telephone book or go online to www.lalecheleague.org. Their website has excellent information. Look under Breastfeeding Info.

Above all, if you are in pain and hating it, **get help**. I know many, many women who continued breastfeeding after a difficult start and ended up having a pleasant experience.

Chapter 15: Breast Pump Basics

There are two types of breast pumps: manual and electric.

Manual Pumps

There are many different manual pumps on the market today. The most popular manual that I know of is the Avent pump. You can use it with one hand. You cover your nipple and areola with the opening of the pump, and you squeeze the handle, to create a suction and simulate the act of breast feeding. The milk goes directly into the baby bottle part of the pump. It is easy to use and is convenient to carry with you. It is also easy to clean. I know many women who have had great success with this pump. Be sure to relax and visualize your baby when you are pumping. You have to feel the "let down" or your milk will just drip out instead of spray out.

Electric Pumps

If you are going back to work, an electric breast pump is a good option. There are now affordably priced electric pumps that are portable and light-weight. Some small-sized electric pumps have double kits that allow you to pump both breasts at once. They often come in carrying cases and are convenient to take to work. I loved having an electric pump. And in case you're wondering, no, they don't hurt!

Some of these pumps may be expensive to buy, but can often be rented on a daily, weekly or monthly rate. I would recommend renting a pump from your local pharmacy before buying one.

The one I used is called the Purely Yours breast pump by Ameda. It is excellent! They are well worth their money; my sister-in-law has it now. I had the Avent manual pump with my first baby and I had the Purely Yours with my second. Both times I just pumped when I wanted to go out and leave the baby with James, or if I wanted to have a couple glasses of wine, I would "pump and dump". I much preferred the electric pump – it was easier and faster.

Making Pumping Easier

This is going to sound weird, but since I have pretty much told you my whole life story, I might as well let it all out. When you are pumping, sometimes it's hard to get the milk to come down. It's like you can't fool your body. So what I did is I would start to pretend (in my mind) that I needed to feed my baby and I would think, "Oh no! My baby is hungry, I really need to feed her!" and my milk would come down. It's sounds really crazy, but it works.

Chapter 16: Your life is about to change completely

When you are pregnant, this is all you ever hear. I am here to tell you that it's true – your life will change, but it will change for the better and you will be shocked at how much you can love this little person. You will wonder how you ever lived without him or her. I often wondered how one little person can make your day so busy, so I will attempt to explain exactly what a typical day is like.

Feedback that I've had from parents suggests that they really liked this part of the book and one woman said, "I was glad to see I wasn't crazy!"

A typical day in the life of a new parent

Below is a typical day in the life of a new mother and father. Let's say the mom's name is Paula and the dad's name is Rick. The baby's name is Walter. He is 6 days old. This is a realistic portrayal of Day 6 postpartum.

6:00am – WAHAHAH. Walter wakes up crying. Paula gets up and picks him up. She is about to nurse him but realizes that she really should go to the bathroom first because he typically nurses for 40 minutes or so. She wakes up Rick ("How could he be sleeping through Walter's screams?" she wonders) and asks him to hold Walter while she goes to the bathroom.

6:04am – Paula takes care of her business, brushes her teeth, thinks about combing her hair but poor Walter is really screaming now.

6:08am – She goes back into their bedroom and asks Rick, "Did you change his diaper?" Rick says, "No, I didn't know you wanted me to...." Frustrated, Paula takes Walter to the change table and changes his diaper. Rick thinks to himself groggily, "Didn't we just change him?"

6:15am – Paula sits down at her nursing station and tries to latch Walter on, but he is still crying so she has to calm him down first. After he calms down she gets him latched on but it's not a good latch and it's hurting Paula. She breaks the latch with her finger and re-latches. She pulls down on his chin to try to get his mouth wide open. It takes a few tries, but eventually she gets him latched on nicely. He nurses like a champ.

6:30am – Suddenly Paula feels as though she will immediately die if she does not have a drink of water. (This really happens.) She yells out to Rick (who is back asleep) and asks him to bring her a glass of water. He brings it to her.

6:40 – Walter has been nursing for 15 minutes and is now sound asleep on Paula's breast. She breaks his latch with her finger and tries to burp him. She has him up on her shoulder and he is still fast asleep. She needs to burp him and wake him up so that she can get him to nurse on the other side. She asks Rick to get up and bring her a cold washcloth. Rick gives up trying to sleep and helps Paula.

6:43 – Rick and Paula try to wake Walter up but he is sound asleep. Eventually, Rick takes Walter to the change table and removes his sleeper, and Walter wakes up.

6:50am – Paula gets Walter latched on the other breast and begins nursing. Walter abruptly starts crying and pulls off her breast. Paula realizes that he probably has gas because she did not get a good burp out of him after the last feed. She tries to burp him in the shoulder position. No burp. She rubs his back, and then she pats his back. Eventually she lays him, tummy down, across her lap and he lets out a good one. Paula gets him latched on again.

7:30am – Paula has finished nursing! She started at 6:00am, an hour and a half ago. (This

- 101 -

is realistic.) Walter is asleep in her arms so she puts him down in his crib. He abruptly wakes up. She feels a "gush" (remember, she is only 6 days postpartum so she is still bleeding) and calls out to Rick to pick up Walter so she can attend to her business in the bathroom.

7:45am – Paula has freshened up and Rick is holding Walter in his arms, rocking in the rocking chair. Paula goes back to bed and Rick stays up with Walter.

8:27am – Walter wakes up with a yell. He's hungry again! Paula got to sleep for 42 minutes.

8:35 – The whole nursing process begins again and takes 1 hour and 10 minutes to complete this time.

9:45am – Paula is starving! She quickly eats a muffin while Rick changes Walter's diaper. They have visitors coming at 10:00am so Paula has a 2-minute shower while Rick changes Walter into a clean outfit.

10:00am – Bob and Sue come over and ooh and ahh over Walter. Walter starts getting fussy (he doesn't like being passed around) after about 15 minutes.

10:30 – Paula realizes that Walter must be hungry again and goes into her room to nurse him. (*By the way, I personally breastfed in front of my visitors but if you don't feel comfortable, just excuse yourself and do what you need to do.)

11:00am – Bob and Sue yell "goodbye" through the door. Paula feels like crying. She barely got to see them at all.

11:15am – Paula and Rick still haven't eaten a proper breakfast. She "wears" Walter in her baby sling (see Resources) and walks around so Walter can fall asleep while Rick makes breakfast.

12:15pm – After breakfast, they decide to go for a walk. As soon as they get their shoes and jackets on, Walter starts to cry. They remove their shoes and jackets, and change his diaper. Paula realizes that he must be hungry again. He eats every two hours, which is normal.

12:30pm – Paula nurses Walter while Rick runs downstairs to do laundry.

1:30pm – After relatching, burping, etc, Walter is finished and they get ready to go out for a walk again. Shoes on, jackets on, and Rick "wearing" Walter this time in the baby sling.

1:37pm – They are outside at last. PTTTTTTHHHSSHHTTTT!! Walter lets out an explosive bowel movement that could be heard around the block. It leaks through all his clothes and through the baby sling. Paula feels like crying again. How frustrating!

2:15pm – Back outside, with Walter in a new outfit and in the stroller this time.

2:30pm – Paula knows that Walter will be hungry soon so she and Rick discuss where to go to nurse him. They go to a nearby bakery.

2:40pm – Paula is discretely nursing Walter at the bakery and feels great for the first time all day. They accomplished a real outing for the first time! Rick runs home to get her another t-shirt because her other breast leaked milk through her shirt and she feels self-conscious.

3:15pm – They head for home.

3:30pm – They arrive home with Walter asleep in the stroller. They leave him in the stroller in the front hall. Paula goes to bed for a nap and Rick sits in the living room where he can see Walter to make sure he doesn't fall out of the stroller.

4:30pm – Walter wakes up hungry again. Rick gets him up and changes his diaper, then brings him to Paula who is still in bed. Paula nurses Walter lying down.

5:30 – Both mom and baby are asleep in bed. Rick is asleep on the couch.

6:30pm – Rick gets up and starts making dinner. Paula and Walter wake up too. Paula changes his diaper.

6:45pm – Paula nurses Walter and eats dinner with one hand.

7:48pm – Paula is finished nursing Walter so she hands him to Rick and goes to the bathroom. Her stitches are bothering her.

8:00pm – Walter is crying and crying and Rick can't seem to settle him. Paula is not feeling relaxed at all.

9:45pm – Rick finally gets Walter to sleep by swaddling him and rocking him to sleep in his arms. Paula is worried because it has been three hours since he last nursed, but he has nursed 7 times today so he's alright. They decide to let him sleep.

10:30pm – Walter wakes up and Paula decides to nurse him in bed so she can rest.

11:30pm – All three of them are asleep in bed.

1:25am – Walter wakes up crying. Paula nurses Walter and they both go back to sleep.

4:00am – Walter wakes up crying. Paula nurses Walter again and spends the next hour trying to get him settled and back to sleep.

5:50am – Paula falls back asleep.

6:30am – Walter wakes up and the next day begins…

Summary:

In this 24-hour period, Paula nursed her new baby 10 times (average is 8 to 10 times in a 24 hour period), his diaper was changed 8 times, and Paula slept a total of 5 hours. She had no time to clean, cook, do laundry or anything else, except to be a great mom to her baby. Rick was a great help! Thank God she has such a supportive partner. Rick got hardly any sleep either and was very attentive to Paula and Walter.

Chapter 17: Frequently Asked Questions

Q: I have no idea what to do with a new baby.

A: Don't worry. Babies are amazing teachers. Day by day, your baby will teach you how to care for her. It can be overwhelming if you think you have to know everything about caring for a baby all at once. You don't have to know everything. When your baby is one day old, you will know what to do with a one-day-old baby. And when she's one week old, you'll know how to care for a one-week-old baby. They are *designed* that way!

Q: I can't imagine having an actual baby in our home.

A: Do you have a pet? It sounds funny, but having a baby is quite similar! You feed it, play with it, and nurture it. You try to anticipate what they need and respond to its cries for attention.

Q: What do I do when the baby cries?

A: See 15 SureFire Ways to Calm Crying

Q: How much does my baby need to sleep?

A: It depends on the baby. Some sleep more than others, some seem to never sleep at all. See the Sleep Chapter in this book. Or read "Healthy Sleep Habits, Happy Child" see Resources.

Q: What's the number one mistake new parents make?

A: They do not realize that their baby is totally overtired or over stimulated and say things like, "My baby doesn't nap." But the baby appears frazzled and wide-eyed. I recommend that all new parents read "Healthy Sleep Habits, Happy Child." – see Resources.

Q: Where should my baby sleep?

A: My babies all started out in our bedroom in a bassinet and then moved on to their own rooms. With Hana, she only lasted about a week in our room and then I shipped her out because she was so noisy! Every peep she made would have me out of bed, checking on her. On the other hand, Alexa was in a bassinet in our room for ten months and so was Trey. Actually, truth be told, Alexa and Trey mostly slept in our bed. I had a bedrail that was made out of mesh and I would put the baby in between me and the bedrail. I often got a full night of sleep! There are so many different options as to where your baby can sleep. Only you and your partner can decide what works best for you two. Others may want to give you advice, but remember, what worked for them may not work for you.

Here are your options:

- Baby in your bed (some people say this is dangerous, but as many as 50% of parents let their child sleep in their bed at some point!)
- Baby in bassinet in your room
- Bedside co-sleeper
- Baby in crib in your room
- Baby in bassinet or crib in their own room
- You and baby in baby's room in another bed (some people set up a bed or futon in the baby's room so that the mother can go in there and nurse in the middle of the night. She usually falls asleep. With this scenario, be careful you don't fall into the trap of not sleeping with your partner anymore).

Q: Should I hold him all the time? Should I just put him down? Where?

A: You can hold him as much as you want. You won't spoil him. And if you're happy doing it, and he's happy, then there's no harm in it. The only problem is that you might get him used to being held all the time and then when you want him to be a little more independent, he will freak out when you try to put him down. You don't need a special "gadget" for him to lay on; he can lay on a receiving blanket on the living room floor or kitchen floor, or wherever, as long as it's safe. Make sure there are no choking hazards around, nor any pets that can harm him. Do not place him on a sofa or bed – even newborn babies can hurtle themselves off!

You may also want to try carrying him in a baby sling. Babies love being carried in this fashion. But be very careful that your baby is getting fresh air while in the sling.

Q: My baby keeps falling asleep when she's nursing! Do I have to wake her up?

A: It depends how long she nursed for, but generally, yes, when they're really little you have to wake them up so they get enough milk. You don't want your baby to have a sip here and a sip there. It's better for her to have a full few ounces at a time. So, you must wake her up. How? Well, some people advocate tickling her foot, or blowing on her face, but my babies could sleep right through that. It sounds kind of mean, but the best method for me was to rub a cold wet cloth on her forehead. She would still be latched on, so I'd wipe her forehead and she'd suddenly perk up and go suck-suck-suck-suck. It she's sound asleep and that doesn't work, you may have to take off her clothes, and diaper and that should do the trick. Keep in mind that she will grow out of this stage eventually! It really only lasts a week or two.

Q: What should I do with my baby when I want to take a shower?

A: This is a great question. If your baby is awake and you leave the room to go have a shower, he will probably feel lonely and start to cry. If you don't mind letting him cry for ten minutes, then it won't hurt him so you can do this. But I didn't. I either showered when my baby was asleep, or I would take her into the bathroom with me. I just put her in the bouncy chair with some toys and I would peek around the shower curtain at her and play peek-a-boo. You can also talk to her or sing songs so she can hear your voice. When babies are under about 8 months old, they don't understand that when you leave them, you will come back again. They think you are gone forever and are never coming back. So it's important to reassure them you are still there.

Q: Why can't I just put a towel down on the bassinet instead of buying special bassinet sheets?

A: This could present a suffocation hazard. What I did sometimes was to place a receiving blanket on my bassinet pad (you can hardly call it a mattress), tuck it under and pin it underneath using diaper pins.

Q: How can I meet other moms?

A: I once met a pregnant woman who said she had no desire to meet other moms and I was quite surprised by this. (She now has an only child with no friends!) When you hang out with other moms, you get a bit of a break because the kids are entertained by each other. It's also great to be able to say, "Has this ever happened to you...?" or "Does your baby do such-and-such...?"

You should check with your local community center to see if they have any "Parent and Tot" or "Baby and Me" drop in groups. The Public Health department often puts them on, and you can go and weigh your baby and talk to a nurse or breastfeeding counselor. Your doctor might also know of new moms' groups in your area. You could also meet new moms at the park, or your public library might have a story time every week. It's never too early to read books to your baby. It's good for you to have a goal to get out of the house every day and it's also really good for your baby to have the stimulation other people's voices and experience new sights and sounds.

You could also check out La Leche League – if this doesn't interest you, you could still call and ask them if they know of any moms' groups in your city. Your church might also have a moms' group. Even if you don't attend a church, you could still call some up and ask around.

Q: What do I need to bring with me when I go out with the baby?

A: Your diaper bag should contain the following items:

- Complete change of clothes (for those explosive poops that cover everything she's wearing. Believe me; it will go right up her back!).
- Four diapers
- Small container of diaper wipes
- Plastic bag for dirty diapers
- Diaper rash cream (if using)
- Extra t-shirt for you if you are nursing (you could leak all over)
- If bottle-feeding, bring a bottle of formula with the powder and sterilized water separate. Even if you are not expecting to be long, it is better to be safe than sorry

and wind up with a hungry, screaming baby and no possible way of feeding her

- Toys for baby
- A bottle of water for you
- Soother or two
- Your wallet, keys, cell phone, etc. You won't be carrying a purse and a diaper bag. Now your diaper bag is your purse.

"There are two lasting bequests we can give our children. One is roots. The other is wings."
~Hodding Carter, Jr.

Chapter 18: Conclusion

I sincerely hope that you have found the information contained in this book to be helpful. I wish you all the best with your new baby. It's true what everyone says about your kids growing up so fast. I can't believe how the time flies. Of course there are those days that seem to last forever, too, and you think you might pull out all your hair!

Enjoy each day, take the good with the bad, know that the challenging times don't last long, and remember that there is no one in the world who knows your baby better than you.

I would also be extremely grateful if you would leave me a review on Amazon. If you search for the title of this book, you should be able to find it easily. It helps me to help more people if I get additional reviews. Thank you in advance.

Sincerely yours,

Suzanne

Suzanne Doyle-Ingram

About The Author

Photo: Visual Hues, Calgary AB

Suzanne Doyle-Ingram is a wife and mother of three young children. She is the bestselling author of many books, some of which were written under a pen name. When she's not busy working full time, or driving her children around, she volunteers at the local food bank. You can connect with Suzanne at: www.SuzanneDoyleIngram.com

Resources

The Best baby books

The Happiest Baby on the Block
By Dr. Harvey Karp

Karp, a pediatrician in Santa Monica, Calif., and assistant professor at the School of Medicine, UCLA, offers a new method to calm and soothe crying infants. While nursing or being held satisfies some babies, others seemingly cry for hours for no reason. These babies suffer from what Karp calls the Fourth Trimester.

This is a great book and there is also a DVD you can get which shows you his way of soothing infants.

Healthy Sleep Habits, Happy Child
by Marc Weissbluth

One of the country's leading researchers updates his revolutionary approach to solving--and preventing--your children's sleep problems.

This is also a very good book that I think every parent should read so they can truly understand children's sleep. It covers how much sleep they need, why they need it, when they need it and how to make it happen.

Here Dr. Marc Weissbluth, a distinguished pediatrician and father of four, offers his groundbreaking program to ensure the best sleep for your child. In Healthy Sleep Habits, Happy Child, he explains with authority and reassurance his step-by-step regime for instituting beneficial habits within the framework of your child's natural sleep cycles.

Secrets of the Baby Whisperer: How to Calm, Connect, and Communicate with Your Baby

by Tracy Hogg

This book became very popular about 10 years ago and many of the points are still valid today. See if you can borrow it from the library.

Tracy Hogg is a neonatal nurse, teacher, and mother of two. She focuses on newborns and their parents, and her simple advice is a blend of intelligent intuition and methods based on her years of experience.

The Baby Book

by James Sears, et al

In their excellent (and hefty) resource guide, *The Baby Book,* attachment parenting specialists William Sears and Martha Sears have provided new parents with their approach to every aspect of baby care basics, from newborns to toddlers. Attachment parenting is a gentle, reasonable approach to parenting that stresses bonding with your baby, responding to her cues, breastfeeding, "wearing" your baby, and sharing sleep with your child.

Websites:

www.lalecheleague.org

www.askdrsears.com

www.breastfeedinginc.ca

62015503R00068

Made in the USA
Middletown, DE
19 January 2018